Third Edition

Social Media and Your Job Search

Maximizing Your Network for a Successful Transition

PURPOSE OF THIS BOOK

This book was written to help transitioning military service members and veterans use social media to increase the effectiveness of their job search. It describes the use of LinkedIn, Facebook, Twitter, and other social media platforms and online tools to help job seekers build their online presence, grow their network of connections, increase their visibility to recruiters and hiring managers, and research career and job opportunities.

To service members transitioning from active duty, and to all U.S. military members, veterans and military spouses: Thank you for your service to our country!

Third Edition

Social Media and Your Job Search

Maximizing Your Network for a Successful Transition

Karin Lockhart-Durkee

 A publication of Corporate Gray

By Karin Lockhart-Durkee
©2020 Competitive Edge Services, Inc.

ISBN 978-0-9996123-3-0

Cover image: MivPiv/iStockphoto
Cover design: Caroline Durkee

Contents

Chapter 1

Why Use Social Media?

Welcome to the 3rd edition of this social media guide, updated to reflect the changes made to social media platforms since the second publication. This book is designed to help you take advantage of valuable social media tools as you prepare for your military-to-civilian career transition.

In this guide you will learn how to build your online professional presence, grow and leverage your network of connections, increase your visibility to recruiters and hiring managers, and research careers and job opportunities.

Although a large portion of this book is focused on using LinkedIn, it also describes how to use Facebook, Twitter, and other social media and online tools in your job search.

Social media platforms are constantly changing, but what remains consistent are the reasons to use social media in your job search: to get noticed, build connections, and find opportunities.

GET NOTICED

According to a recent recruiting survey by Jobvite.com, 94% of recruiters said they are using or plan to use social media to find prospective job candidates, with LinkedIn being the site used most by recruiters.

As more recruiters are using social media to search for candidates, there is evidence it is working for them. The survey showed that 89% of recruiters reported having successfully hired a candidate who was identified or introduced through LinkedIn.

If you want to be found by recruiters, it helps tremendously to have a social media presence. This guide will show you how to increase your professional online presence, or digital footprint, thereby increasing your chances of getting noticed and ultimately getting hired.

BUILD CONNECTIONS

Close to 80%, of jobs are landed through networking. And employers often report that their employee referrals are the best source of quality hires. It is who you know that will lead to an initial look followed by an interview and job offer. And who you know will grow exponentially through an active presence on social media sites such as LinkedIn.

It's not enough to create a fabulous online profile, only to let it collect dust. You need to use these sites to make meaningful connections. The beauty of social media is the ease with which you can grow a relevant network right from your computer -- connecting to colleagues, recruiters, experts and influencers in your industry to help get your foot in the door of opportunities.

These sites allow you to connect worldwide, which is particularly helpful to military members on assignment overseas who are preparing to transition to a civilian job, or for those who will be relocating after they leave the military.

This book will show you how to connect to colleagues and experts with whom you have something in common. Your network becomes a huge support group for your job search. For instance, transitioning military members who connect with fellow veterans can experience a wealth of job search and transition support through that network. Your fellow veterans have been through the transition and are often willing to help you through the process, just as you will be willing to help others following in your footsteps down the road.

FIND OPPORTUNITIES

Social media sites can help you discover job and career opportunities you may not have known about otherwise. They are also a useful resource for researching companies, recruiters, and job openings. Doing careful research before attending a job fair or interview will help you make the most of the event or make a good first impression at an interview.

WEIGH THE BENEFIT

Are privacy concerns making you hesitant to join the social media revolution? This is a valid concern, especially if you hold a security clearance like many military and government personnel. There are differing views about whether cleared individuals should be using social media and whether they should disclose a clearance in their profile. See more on that in the next chapter.

Ultimately, this is your decision and as mentioned in the next chapters, you should take advantage of the privacy controls of each platform and set them as appropriate for your comfort level. If you are careful about what you post and keep your focus and content professional, these social media sites can be a valuable asset to your job search.

In this book you'll see how to put these social media tools to work for your military-to-civilian job search. Read on to learn how easy it is to create your professional online presence and build a supportive and beneficial network.

Chapter 2

Account Security & Privacy

It is important to consider the privacy and security of your online accounts, and this is especially true for your social media accounts, as they contain information about your experience and background.

BASIC SECURITY
Here are some basic rules that you should apply to any online account:
• Change your password every couple of months.
• Use strong passwords, such as a password phrase at least 12 characters long, including a mixture of upper and lower case, special characters, and numbers.
• Enable two-step verification when available.
• Sign out of your account after you use a publicly shared computer.
• Beware of phishing. For example, make sure a recruiter's email address matches their company's online domain name (website URL) before sharing your resume or personal information with them.

PRIVACY SETTINGS
The first step in setting up any social media account should be to familiarize yourself with the account and privacy settings. Login and explore all of the available options. If you don't understand a setting, learn about it from that

platform's help center or find more about it by searching the Internet.

It is important to explore all the options and select your setting preferences based on several considerations. The first is to make sure you follow the social media policies that your current employer (the branch of service or agency where you work) has in place. Learn what those rules arc so you can comply.

The second consideration is your personal comfort level. However, you should balance this with the third consideration: the ability for recruiters to find you. Setting your account privacy too conservatively will keep recruiters who are not in your network (which is all, if you are new to the social media platform) from seeing your profile. You want to be easily found by recruiters searching for candidates with your skills and expertise.

SENSITIVE INFORMATION

It is common for military members to have classified or sensitive information in their background. Many hold a security clearance and have worked on classified projects or in sensitive locations.

Make sure you know what is allowed to be shared, and be cautious about what you post online. There is no balancing here -- if it is classified or sensitive, do not share it. This could include locations, project names, office size, budget amounts, and any other such details. Highlight your skills without revealing sensitive information.

You can state that you have a clearance and the type, and this will help you get noticed by recruiters searching for cleared candidates. Any other details about clearance should be saved for the face-to-face job interview.

There is more information and advice about account security and privacy settings in the chapters that follow.

Chapter 3

LinkedIn: Your Professional Online Presence

As LinkedIn is the largest professional online network, it is an important site to use for your job search and for your career. This chapter covers using LinkedIn to create your professional online presence through building your profile and showing your expertise.

According to the recent Jobvite survey, of those recruiters hiring from a social network or social media, 94% had hired through LinkedIn. Since it is the social media site used most by recruiters to find candidates, it is definitely where you want to establish a presence.

This chapter steps you through using LinkedIn to build your online professional portfolio to showcase and share your expertise.

GETTING STARTED

If you are new to LinkedIn, creating an account begins by going to www.linkedin.com, clicking the Join Now link, and entering your name, email and password. The email you use to set-up your account will be set as your primary email. You can add more email addresses to your account later, and reassign the primary as needed. After verifying your email address, you'll be stepped through the process of creating your profile.

Following the advice in this chapter will help you build a complete but concise and effective profile that will help you get noticed by recruiters who are searching for candidates with your skills and experience.

PRIVACY SETTINGS

Although this was mentioned in the previous chapter, this is a reminder to explore the Settings & Privacy section the next time you login to your LinkedIn account, and revisit these settings often, as the options can change.

These settings are accessed by clicking the **Me** thumbnail photo icon in the top menu bar, then select **Settings & Privacy** in the drop-down list. Navigate through the Account, Privacy, and Communications tabs to explore all the options and select your preferences.

One of the items under Privacy lets you set your job seeking preferences. This gives you the option to signal that you are open to opportunities, share your profile with the recruiter who posted a job of interest, and more. Click on every privacy setting to make sure you have all the options set the way you want them.

ACCOUNT SETTINGS

As mentioned earlier, you can have multiple email addresses aligned with your LinkedIn account. Your primary email address is the one you used to create the account. If you have other email addresses, you can align them all with your account. This will allow others to find you when they search by an email that is not your primary. You can change which email is designated as the primary from your account settings.

Also from your account settings page, you can setup the two-step verification, and you can change your password regularly. If you are logged in from a publicly shared computer, be sure to log out of your LinkedIn account when done. Closing the browser does not necessarily log you out. To double check it, reopen the browser and go to LinkedIn again to make sure you have been properly logged out.

TURN OFF ACTIVITY BROADCASTS

If you are making many changes to your profile, you can turn off your activity broadcasts. This way every edit you make won't be announced to your network. You can turn this off under your Privacy settings so you are not sharing your job changes, education changes, etc.

Turn this back to "Yes" when you are done making major changes to your profile. That way your activity and updates will once again show up to your connections. It's good stay on people's radar, as a rule of thumb -- you want to get noticed!

BUILD AN EFFECTIVE LINKEDIN PROFILE

Now let's get to building your LinkedIn profile, which will really become your professional portfolio. A complete and well-constructed LinkedIn profile is the first step in getting noticed. Click **View profile** from the drop-down list under the **Me** icon in the menu bar to edit your profile.

The following suggestions will help make your LinkedIn profile professional, effective, and searchable. Including relevant keywords and phrases in your profile sections, ones that describe your skills, experience, achievements and goals, will make you more likely to come up in the search results of recruiters and hiring managers. How do you determine those keywords? Read on!

And it goes without saying (but I'm saying it anyway) that you should check and double check your profile for proper spelling and grammar, just as you would your resume. Use a program with a spell and grammar checker, like Microsoft Word, to prepare the text, then copy and paste the error-free wording into your LinkedIn profile.

UPLOAD A PHOTO

Including your photo on your profile will add credibility and help others make a more personal connection to you. Having a profile photo increases the likelihood of your profile being viewed and your invitations to connect accepted. Invest in a professionally taken photo, as you can use the picture across all your social media networks to be consistent and recognizable.

Your photo should be a good quality headshot (from the waist up or elbows up) with a clean background and free of distractions (no hat, sunglasses, pets, or other people). It should show you looking professional and friendly.

Keep in mind that your photo will not only be seen when someone views your profile, but in many other places on LinkedIn, such as next to your endorsements and recommendations of others, your posted discussions, and your comments in groups.

You can also upload a background image at the top of your profile to add visual interest and branding. This could be something relevant to your industry or expertise, or an image that reflects your professional character. Check the LinkedIn help center for current profile and background image size guidelines.

CUSTOMIZE YOUR PROFILE URL

LinkedIn allows you to customize your public profile URL, which is the web address for your LinkedIn profile. The URL was automatically generated when you created your account and contains random characters after your name (to ensure it is unique) that you can remove and improve.

Your public profile URL is the address you see at the top of your browser when you are viewing your profile. If you have not yet customized it, click the **Edit public profile & URL** link to the right of your profile. This will allow you to customize the URL and will show you the options available for your public profile visibility.

Click the pencil icon next to your URL. Remove the random characters after your name. This makes it a cleaner and more recognizable address to share, whether it's on your resume, in your email signature, or on your business card.

For example, my original public profile URL that was automatically generated by LinkedIn ended something like this: /karin-durkee-5q013a17. I customized it to end with /karindurkee, which is easier to read and remember, and it looks more professional. If your name is already taken, you could add your middle initial to it, or add a number or a professional acronym after your name, like PMP, RN, or CISSP. Think recognizable (your name) and professional (add an acronym) as needed to make it unique. Once you've customized and started sharing your profile URL, don't change it again, or the link you previously shared will be broken.

YOUR PROFILE VISIBILITY

Below the URL customization, you'll see the options to choose who can view your profile on LinkedIn. You can also select what parts of your profile will show on Internet search engines. These settings are for the public version of your profile outside of LinkedIn. When considering your profile visibility, keep in mind that you want people in your industry and recruiters who are not necessarily in your network to be able to view your profile.

CREATE AN EFFECTIVE HEADLINE

Your Headline is an important first impression that shows what you are about. Why should a recruiter take a closer look at your profile? Tell them in the headline. Don't just use the headline that LinkedIn populates by default, which is your current job title and employer. And use the 120 character limit wisely to make your headline count.

Create a descriptive headline that not only shows your industry and area of expertise, but that also reflects the most relevant skills (keywords and phases) recruiters are searching for in a candidate.

Use your resume, if you've already created one, to identify your skills and expertise to populate your headline and the other sections of your profile. But don't stop there. More research is required to make sure you are including the most relevant keywords and phrases to the jobs you are targeting.

RESEARCH KEYWORDS & PHRASES
Search job postings for the job descriptions and the skills that recruiters list as being required and preferred. You can learn a lot from these job postings about which skills are most relevant and what the recruiters will be searching for in candidates.

Copy the description and skills list from several appropriate job postings and paste them into a word cloud generator (search for word cloud generators on the Internet, as there are many free ones available). This will create a word cloud that shows the words in varying sizes depending on how often they appear in the text. You can visualize the words and phrases mentioned most often in those job posts, which are likely the most relevant skills. If you have those skills, then include those keywords and phrases in your headline, summary, and other sections of your profile. If you don't have a skill or certification that seems to be important in the job listings, be proactive in acquiring it before you leave the military.

Researching the job postings will help you select the proper terminology that your target audience (the recruiter) will understand. Always keep your target audience in mind when deciding how to word the sections of your profile. Recruiters might not have an extensive knowledge of military terms and acronmyms. If this is the case, you need to translate your military jargon and acronyms into civilian language they will understand, can relate to, and will be searching for.

It is recommended that if you are retiring from the military, use the term "transitioning" instead, as this has a more positive connotation in the civilian workplace. For additional help choosing the right language, consider using a military-to-civilian skills translator to match your military skills to the civilian keywords that recruiters would be more likely to use. Several military-to-civilian skills translators can be found by searching the Internet.

Here are some sample headlines that convey relevant skills, industries, areas of expertise, and professional goals:

Aviation Electronics Technician with Management experience transitioning from Navy

Army Supply Chain Engineer with 20+ years in Logistics Program Management/Supply Chain Management/ Procurement

Transitioning Army Information Security Officer with CISSP seeking position as an Industrial Security Professional

Also research others on LinkedIn to see what they've included in their headline and summary. What is their work experience and education? Search for people that have the job you want at the company where you want to work, and learn from their profiles. While you are viewing their profile, invite them to join your network. Searching for relevant people and sending invitations to connect are covered in detail in the next chapter.

YOUR LOCATION

Include your location on your profile. This is not your physical address, it is the area where you live and want to work. If you plan to relocate when you transition, and you are looking for a job in a different location from where you are now, select that new location on your profile. You could mention in your summary that you are currently in location A but plan to relocate to B when you transition.

LinkedIn will use your location to help recruiters find you, even if the recruiter did not enter a location in their search criteria. You are more likely to come up in a recruiter's search if your location matches theirs.

YOUR CONTACT INFO

Next to your location in your profile is a link for you to edit your contact information. Click the **Contact info** link to view and edit the information your network can access from your profile. Complete only the contact information that you are comfortable sharing with others on LinkedIn. Your primary email address is automatically included in this information, but it is only visible to your 1st degree connections (those who you've invited to connect or you've accepted their invitations to connect). The degrees of your network connections are explained in the next chapter.

YOUR SUMMARY

The About section of your profile is also referred to as your summary. This is where you can tell your story and highlight your strengths. This write-up is less formal than your resume and should be written in first person, as though you are talking to the reader. This summary should support what you have in your headline and expand on it.

Describe your expertise and accomplishments, and let your passion show through. Use keywords and phrases from your research that you know are important for the jobs you are targeting and that recruiters will likely be looking for.

If you are starting on a new career path, it might be difficult to match your skills to a completely new occupation. If so, focus on the transferable skills you acquired from your military service (e.g. leadership, team work, strong work ethic, decision making in adverse conditions) that transfer across disciplines.

As mentioned earlier in this book, if you include that you have a security clearance in your summary, it is not recommended that you disclose anything but the clearance type. Be cautious about what you include in your profile that might be considered sensitive. Highlight your skills without revealing sensitive information. Focusing on your skills will help you fill in gaps where you are unable to describe specific projects or details about your experience.

Keep your summary short and to the point. A good length is 2-3 paragraphs with 2-3 sentences in each. Only the first few lines of your summary will show in your About section, and the reader will have to click "Read more" to see the rest. With that in mind, put your most relevant skills up front in the first few sentences.

Include in the summary your professional goals and future business ambitions. Also include a list of your

"Expertise:" or "Specialities:" at the end. These could be in a paragraph separated by commas or as a bulleted list that highlights your most relevant skills and keywords.

YOUR FEATURED SECTION

The Featured section of your profile lets you transform your profile into a professional portfolio. You can highlight discussions and articles you've posted on LinkedIn, links to web content, and documents. More on sharing documents in the next section.

To add the featured section to your profile, click the **Add profile section** button and click **Featured** from the drop-down list.

ADD LINKS & DOCUMENTS

You can add links, documents, photos, videos, or presentations not only to your featured section, but also to the other sections of your profile to enrich each section. Add these by clicking the pencil edit icon next to the section, then scroll down to the "Media" part of the editor to enter a link or upload a file. Make the title of the link or file descriptive, so someone viewing your profile will know the item is of interest to them.

The content of the documents you upload to your profile is not searchable by LinkedIn, so do not use these documents as a substitute for including keywords and phrases in your profile. However, the documents can be used to showcase your professional work and are viewable to someone browsing your profile.

UPLOAD YOUR RESUME

Uploading multiple versions of your resume can provide tailored views of your skills, background and expertise. Your profile encompasses all of your skills, but attaching tailored versions of your resume will give a recruiter easy access to a focused synopsis of your skills. Remember to use descriptive titles to characterize each resume.

YOUR EXPERIENCE & EDUCATION

Add your current and past employers and education to your profile. If you have a resume, use it to complete these sections. Include the most relevant keywords in the job titles, and include a brief description of each company with bullets of your skills and accomplishments.

If you don't have a resume created yet, don't let that stop you from creating your profile. Start with your latest accomplishments, and you can add the rest later as you build your resume. Your online profile is a work in progress that you can constantly build on and improve.

If a past job has nothing to do with your current career field, list it with a short description, using those transferable skills to describe your duties and responsibilities. Listing all your past employers and education will help you find connections and opportunities and build your network. LinkedIn uses your profile content to suggest people you may know, jobs and companies you may be interested in, and relevant groups to join.

SKILLS & ENDORSEMENTS

Add keywords and phrases in the Skills & Endorsements section that are relevant to your career field. The skills listed in your profile work like tags, increasing your search potential within LinkedIn. This should be the list of your strengths, because others in your network will be endorsing the skills that you list here. You can add up to 50 skills, but consider keeping it to 15-25 of your most relevant skills. If the list is too long, the relevant skills can get lost in the noise.

Skills that have the most endorsements appear first, and skills without endorsements appear based on how recently they were added. You don't have to keep the default order of your skills. Click the pencil edit icon in that section, then click and drag the move icon (four horizontal lines) to reorder your skills. Pin your top three skills to the top by clicking the pin icon next to them.

Getting at least one endorsement for a skill will increase your chances of coming up in someone's search by that skill. When you are endorsed for a skill you have listed, the endorsement will be automatically added. If it is a skill not included in your list, LinkedIn will give you the option of adding that skill. Keep your list of skills relevant to the career path you plan to take.

Endorse your 1st degree connections for the skills that you have in common. This could make you appear on their profile as being experienced in that skill.

RESEARCH OTHER PROFILES

It's worth mentioning again how much you can learn from viewing the profiles of colleagues and others in your career field to get ideas on what skills and keywords to use throughout your profile. Search for people on LinkedIn who have the same job title as you, as well as those who have the job you hope to land. Click their name from the search results to view their profile and see what education and past work experience they have. What groups did they join? Who are they connected to? You'll find useful information for enhancing your profile by studying what others include.

ADD SECTIONS

Add a section to your profile by clicking the **Add profile section** button. Click **Background** and **Accomplishments** to see the options for additional sections. Select a section like certifications, projects, awards, languages, organizations, and more, that will help round out your profile and showcase your skills.

For example, add the organizations section if you are a member of a professional organization, and add the projects or publications sections to show your professional expertise. If you've done volunteer work, be sure to add the volunteer experience section and describe your skills and achievements from this work.

GET RECOMMENDATIONS

Ask for recommendations from people in your network. Click on **Add profile section** and then **Request a recommendation** from the drop-down list. LinkedIn will prompt you to enter a connection and create a message requesting a brief recommendation for your profile.

In your message, provide the recipient a short description of your work duties and successes to make it easy for them to write about you. Include any specific projects or information you want them to mention.

You can also request a recommendation from someone in your 1st degree network from their profile page. Click the **More...** icon on their profile, then select **Request a recommendation** from the drop-down list. You can easily reciprocate by also selecting **Recommend**.

A good rule is to have two to three recommendations from managers, supervisors, and colleagues for each job listed in the Experience section of your profile. Also get recommendations from professors if you are a student and from those for whom you've done volunteer work. If you're in a leadership position, get recommendations from people who work for you, and reciprocate.

Offer thoughtful recommendations to colleagues or

classmates who you've worked with and respect. Giving and reciprocating recommendations goes a long way toward building relationships.

REORDER THE SECTIONS

You don't have to keep the default order in which the sections appear on your profile. You can change the order of the sections as appropriate to feature the most relevant parts of your profile.

Click and drag the move icon (four horizontal lines) of the section you want rearranged to move it up or down in your profile. This allows you to place your most relevant sections prominently at the top of your profile.

For instance, if you speak multiple languages and that is most important for the job you are targeting, move the Languages section up near the top of your profile. Or if you just earned a degree that is the top criterion for the job you are targeting, move the Education section above your Experience section.

BACK-UP YOUR PROFILE

You can save your LinkedIn profile as a neatly formatted PDF to back it up and also to share it. Click the **More...** button and select **Save to PDF** from the drop-down list. You worked hard to create a professional profile, so share the PDF with recruiters and others who are helping you with your job search. Attach the PDF to emails or print it out to include with your job applications, as appropriate.

BROADCAST TO YOUR NETWORK

Once you are done building your profile, turn on your activity broadcasts from the privacy settings. This will allow your future updates to be seen by your network as you share content and build your online reputation.

SHARE YOUR EXPERTISE

Building your profile is not the only way of getting noticed and showing your expertise on LinkedIn. You can share your knowledge and establish yourself as an expert in your industry by posting discussions, sharing links to articles of interest, and publishing articles or papers you have written.

Post discussions on your home page regularly to stay active with your network. A post might be as simple as sharing a link to an article you found interesting. By posting and sharing information about your industry, you start to establish yourself as an expert. Be sure to like and share posts of others in your network as well.

GET PUBLISHED

LinkedIn has a feature that lets you publish your own articles, white papers, advice column, etc. online. It's like being a guest blogger on LinkedIn rather than having to set-up your own blog (blogging is mentioned in a later chapter, for those who love to write).

You can post an article to LinkedIn from your home page. Click the **Write an article** link below **Start a post**. Type the headline (title), then copy and paste the body of the article from the Word or similar program where you wrote it. The formatting icons let you adjust the text and add hyperlinks and media to the content.

Include an image (optional, but recommended) to draw attention and add interest to your article. You can also tag your post with relevant industries, skills, and other keywords before you publish, to help people find it.

After you click **Publish,** your published post will show on your LinkedIn profile in the Activity section and will be broadcast to your network. You can share the post on LinkedIn, Facebook, or Twitter by clicking the share icon (curved arrow) at the bottom of a published post.

Chapter 4

LinkedIn: Your Professional Network

Now that you have an effective LinkedIn profile, you can use this large professional network to build your own network of relevant connections. Your profile and network are interdependent -- an effective profile helps you find connections, and growing your network increases the likelihood that your profile will show up at the top of search results, leading to more opportunities.

CHECK YOUR SETTINGS

It's worth mentioning again that you should check your account settings often to make sure everything is set the way you want. Check your Account, Privacy and Communications settings. If you don't understand an option, search the LinkedIn Help Center for an explanation of it. The Help Center can be accessed by clicking the **Me** thumbnail photo icon in the top menu bar and selecting **Help** from the drop-down list.

DEGREES OF CONNECTION

Your LinkedIn network is built on different degrees of connections. When you view someone else's profile, you'll see a 1st, 2nd, or 3rd next to their name that shows their degree of connection to you, if any.

Your 1st degree connections are those who have accepted your invitation to join your network, or you've accepted their invitation. All of their 1st degree connections are now in your 2nd degree. Your 3rd degree are all the people connected to your 2nd degree. What?! For example, let's say Sue is connected to John who's connected to Paul. If Sue accepts your invitation to connect, John is now in your 2nd level, and Paul is in your 3rd level.

If you are in one or more groups with someone but have no other connection to them, they are still considered part of your network, since you have a group in common. Groups are a great way to expand your network, but more on that later in this chapter.

FIND CONNECTIONS

Find people to connect with by searching your email address book or by adding connections through your present/past colleagues and classmates. LinkedIn helps you find these connections based on your profile information (another good reason to fill out your profile completely). Click **My Network** in the menu bar, and browse the suggestions of **People you may know**.

If you see someone you want to invite, click on their name to first visit their profile and connect from there. Clicking the **Connect** button from the list of suggestions will send the default invitation without letting you customize it (more on customizing invitations coming up). Make it a goal to invite new connections to join your network every time you visit LinkedIn.

USE YOUR EMAIL CONTACTS

A quick and easy way to begin building your network is to import your email address book to LinkedIn from the **Add personal contacts** link on your **My Network** page.

LinkedIn will import your email contacts and allow you to send invitations to join your network to those contacts.

Manage your list of imported contacts, rather than just clicking "Select all" which would send an invitation to everyone. Select each person that it makes sense for you to invite to your network. It also includes your email contacts that are not currently on LinkedIn, and you can send them an invitation to join LinkedIn and your network. Again, pick and choose only the relevant contacts to invite.

FIND ALUMNI

You can find classmates and fellow alumni to connect with on your school's LinkedIn page. Use the search box to find your school and visit the official school page. On the left side of the page, click **Alumni,** then scroll down to browse the alumni who share a connection with you.

Also search for alumni by **Where they live, Where they work**, and by clicking the **Next** arrow to page through more filters. Find classmates close to your year group by entering a start year and end year in the boxes above the search filters. This can also help you find more seasoned alumni who might be good mentors.

After running the search, scroll to the bottom to see the returned alumni. Click the **Connect** button below someone's name to invite them to join your network. Be sure to click **Add a note** to personalize the invitation (described later). Reach out to your fellow alumni for information about their company and possibly for a referral to their hiring manager.

PEOPLE SEARCH

The search box at the top of every page helps you find people, jobs, companies, and more. When you click inside the search box, the drop-down list lets you choose the category of your search. Select one of the categories (people, jobs, content, companies, schools or groups), or type in your keywords without selecting a category to search all.

To search for people, select **People** from the options. Then click the **All filters** link to view and apply more filters for an advanced search. Scroll through all the filter options to narrow and customize your search.

Use the **Current companies** filter to find people who work at a company where you would like to work. Learn from their profiles and reach out to them for insights and information about their company.

FIND FELLOW VETERANS

As a transitioning service member, one of the greatest resources for your transition and future career is your network of fellow military veterans. Make it a priority to connect with other veterans not only on LinkedIn, but also through veteran websites and military associations, which is covered in more detail in a later chapter. The value of this support group cannot be stressed enough.

To find fellow veterans to connect with on LinkedIn, use the **Past companies** filter. Type in the branch of service, for example US Army, in the **Past companies** box. You can add multiple past companies to a search.

You must type in the branch of service as it appears on the official LinkedIn company page, or it will not appear as an option in the drop-down list. The official names on LinkedIn for these branches are: US Army, United States Air Force, US Navy, United States Marine Corps, and U.S. Coast Guard. When in doubt, search for the company page first and note how the name appears. Once your search criteria have been selected, click **Apply** to run the search.

MAKE THE CONNECTION

Once you've found people to add to your network, you can connect with them in several ways. The method for connecting with an individual varies depending on your network relationship. The three degrees of separation work as follows.

If they are in your 1st degree, you are already connected and you can send them a message by clicking the **Message** button in your search results or in their profile.

If they are in your 2nd degree or in a group with you, you'll see the **Connect** button instead of Message. Click Connect, or click their name to be taken to their profile and click Connect from there. In the pop-up box that appears when you click Connect, click **Add a note** and add a sentence to personalize the invitation (see more on personalizing your invitations below).

If they are in your 3rd degree and their full last name and the Connect button are showing, you can connect with them in the same way as above.

If they are in your 3rd degree and just the first initial of their last name appears, or if they are out of your network, the Connect button is not an option, but you can contact them through **InMail**.

InMail is a private message that enables you to contact a LinkedIn user directly who is not in your network. This is a paid feature that you can purchase individually or as part of an upgraded account. If you don't receive an InMail response in seven days, LinkedIn will allow you to send another InMail.

PERSONALIZE YOUR INVITATIONS

A good habit is to invite people to connect with you from their profile page or from the search results, but not from the list of "People you may know" on your My Network page. When you click the Connect button from someone's profile page or from your search results, you will get the pop-up box that lets you personalize the invitation. If you click the Connect button from the "People you may know" list, the default invitation will be sent without allowing you to add a personal message.

Click **Add a note** in the invitation pop-up box. Type a sentence or two to introduce yourself and let them know why you are a relevant connection. For example, "I am transitioning from the Army in a few months and am interested in learning more about your company. Please join my network."

Personalized invitations are more likely to be accepted. An invitation has a character limit of 299, so be brief in telling them why you chose to invite them to your network (what it is you have in common). A thoughtful, personal message is the best way to establish a new connection.

PEOPLE YOU MAY KNOW

LinkedIn will suggest people you may know based on the work experience, education, skills, and other information that you've included in your profile. These suggestions can be helpful and provide an easy way to make relevant connections.

Browse LinkedIn's suggestions for growing your network found on your **My Network** page. If you see someone you want to connect with, click their name to go to their profile. From their profile you can click **Connect**, and you'll get the pop-up box that let's you personalize your invitation.

YOUR PENDING INVITATIONS

A red number on the **My Network** link in the menu bar signals that you have that number of invitations pending your response. Check your pending invitations regularly, and take timely action by clicking Accept or Ignore for each.

The person's photo, name, and headline are visible from the pending list, as well as their message if they included one. This could be enough information for you to determine whether you want to accept or ignore them. If it's not apparent from that information, click their name to go to their profile to help you make a more informed decision to accept or ignore.

If you accept an invitation, the sender receives an email from LinkedIn letting them know that you are now in their network. If you ignore an invitation, the person is not notified, you are quietly removed from their pending sent invitations list, and they are removed from your pending list. It is okay to ignore invitations if you do not see the relevance of the connection. You are in control of your 1st degree connections. And if you have a clearance, be especially careful about who you connect with.

If you accept a connection and later regret the decision, you can remove someone from your network. On the **My Network** page, click **Connections** to view the list of all your 1st degree connections. Start typing a name or use the **Search with filters** link to find someone in your network. Click the three vertical dots icon to remove that connection. They are not notified that you removed them.

Remember to keep your 1st degree connections relevant. It is not all about the numbers and growing a large network, it is about growing a relevant network. The size will grow over time exponentially as you add a few good connections at a time.

REACH OUT TO YOUR CONNECTIONS

Access your list of 1st degree connections from the **Connections** link on the **My Network** page. You can filter your list of connections by clicking **Search with filters** and then **All filters** to run a focused people search, as explained earlier, except this search will be on only your 1st degree connections.

Search your 1st degree connections, because these are people who you can Message on LinkedIn. Reach out to them for advice on your transition or information about their current company. You've already determined these connections are relevant, or they would not be in your 1st degree network. Now you can put that relevant network to good use in your job search.

DOWNLOAD YOUR CONNECTIONS

You can access a copy of your account data, 1st degree connections and more from your Privacy settings. Go to your **Settings and privacy** page, click **How LinkedIn uses your data**, then click **Get a copy of your data**. You many be prompted to sign-in again.

Select the data files you want to download, such as your connections, then click **Request archive**. You will receive an email from LinkedIn when the zipped file is ready to be downloaded. The file of your connections may include contacts' email addresses, depending on if they had changed the "Who can download your email" privacy option to allow 1st connections to download their email.

JOIN RELEVANT GROUPS

By joining groups on LinkedIn, you will tap into a large community of veterans, employers, military members, and industry leaders. Joining relevant groups will help you grow a meaningful network exponentially.

Fellow group members are similar to a 2nd degree connection. You can invite them to join your network, and you can contact them through the group. Click the three dots at the top right of someone's group discussion to message that person.

You can join up to 100 groups on LinkedIn. Groups let you find people with similar interests, share content, get answers, learn about job opportunities, and make valuable business connections.

FIND GROUPS

Use the LinkedIn search box to search for veteran and industry groups. Select **Groups** when running the search. Search by keywords like military veterans, transitioning military, as well as terms relevant to your industry.

After doing a group search, click the group name to view the group, then click the **Join** or **Request to join** link. Depending on the group's settings, you will either be automatically accepted, or the group manager will review your profile to see if you meet their membership criteria.

Unlisted groups will not show up in a search. You can join an unlisted group by invitation from the group owner or manager, or by requesting to join after receiving the link to the group.

CONTRIBUTE TO GROUP CONVERSATIONS

Listen, learn and engage in group conversations. If you are new to a group, read what others are discussing to get a feel for it. When you have something to contribute, add a comment to a conversation. Or "like" a conversation to show you appreciate their post. This is a simple way to get on someone's radar.

Start your own discussions, ask questions, offer advice, and share insights to establish your presence and demonstrate your expertise. This will help you make valuable connections while building your personal brand.

Click on a group member's name to go to their profile. If you see the **Connect** button, click it to send them an invitation (and be sure to personalize it). If the Connect button is not an option, select **Follow** from the **More...** button to follow the person and see their updates. Or you can send them an InMail (as described earlier).

You can view and manage your list of groups by clicking the **Work** icon in the top right on the menu bar, then click **Groups** from the drop-down box. Click a group name to visit the group, or click the three vertical dots icon to adjust your group settings or leave the group. Manage your notifications from the group by clicking the bell icon on the group page.

USE YOUR GROUP CONNECTIONS

Connect individually with people you meet in a group. Invite them to join your network and message them as mentioned earlier. This will allow you to continue the conversations outside the group and build relationships.

To the right of the group page you'll see the write-up about the group and the group's admins. You will also see the members of the group. Click the **See all** link to browse and search the members.

Groups can be excellent resources for information, so take advantage of all that they offer in growing your network, learning from others, and expanding your reach.

START YOUR OWN GROUP

If you are passionate about a subject in your industry, for example, and haven't found an existing group that covers it the way you would like, consider starting your own LinkedIn group. From your list of **Groups** that you can access under the **Work** icon, there is button to **Create group**. Share your new group with your network, inviting connections to join it from the **Manage** link.

NETWORK IN PERSON

The LinkedIn mobile app has a feature that can help you grow your in-person network. Before going to your next in-person networking event, such as a job fair or professional association mixer, download the LinkedIn app to your smartphone and login to your account.

When you arrive at the event, open the LinkedIn app and turn on the **Find nearby** feature. Do this by clicking **My Network** on the app, and depending on the device, click the **Find nearby** link or click the silhouette with a plus sign icon to access the **Find nearby** link.

Anyone else in the room who has also turned on this feature will show up on your app and you on theirs. Click to invite them to join your network, and they can accept your invitation (or vice versa). There is more information about using the LinkedIn mobile apps in the next chapter.

POST UPDATES

As mentioned in the previous chapter, posting discussions on your home page keeps you active and engaged with your network. Share insights, making sure your activity broadcasts are turned on from your Settings & Privacy page. Post updates and announcements about your job search, interesting articles, and thoughts and questions relevant to your industry that are aligned with your professional goals. Also post discussions in your groups.

Your network will grow as you become more engaged in discussions that matter to you. You'll find yourself connecting with interesting and knowledgeable professionals. If you share it, they will come.

Chapter 5

LinkedIn: Research and Opportunities

LinkedIn can be a valuable research tool to help you find job and career opportunities. Use it to investigate companies and careers, search for and apply to jobs, and prepare for job fairs and interviews.

LinkedIn will do some of the work for you, suggesting relevant jobs and companies for you based on the information in your profile. But there's more work to be done and much to be discovered.

COMPANY RESEARCH

If you are unsure what companies to target, browse LinkedIn's suggestions that you'll find by clicking **Jobs** in the menu bar. Since these are based on the information in your profile, you'll likely find relevant companies that were not previously on your radar.

Gather information on specific companies that you are targeting and on their employees. The more you can learn about them, the richer your job search will be. There are several ways to find this information:

FOLLOW COMPANIES

Search for and follow a company on LinkedIn to receive the company's updates on your home page. This will keep you informed about what the company is posting. Add filters to your company search, such as location, industry, and size.

To find a specific company, select **Companies** from the search box drop-down list, then type the company name in the search box. Go to the company's page by clicking their name in the search results. On their page you can **Follow** them, which shows your interest in the organization and could put you on their radar. Another way to get noticed by a company is to like, comment on, or share their posts.

VISIT COMPANY PAGES

Visit LinkedIn company pages to get information about companies and their employees. View the company's job opportunities from their Careers page. You can also see what services they offer and if there are any groups featured by that company.

See which of your connections work at the company. A link to those connections is on the right side of the company page. Click the link to view the full list of your connections to that company. Send your 1st degree connections a message to let them know you are interested in working for their company. They probably won't be in a hiring position, and you're not asking them for a job. But they could provide you with information about the company and give you advice on pursuing a job there.

RESEARCH EMPLOYEES

Study employees' profiles to see what skills, experience, and education they possess and what positions they hold. This will help you determine if you are qualified for the same or similar positions at that company.

RESEARCH RECRUITERS

Research recruiters or hiring managers before they interview you. Check out their LinkedIn profiles to learn about their backgrounds and see if you have anything in common (school, interests, connections). This is a great way to establish a rapport, and it also shows them you did your homework in preparing for the interview.

FIND JOBS

You'll see LinkedIn's suggestions for jobs and companies by clicking the **Jobs** tab in the menu bar. Browse the suggestions that are listed in the **Based on your profile** section. Click on those of interest to learn more about the job and company.

Search for jobs using the search box and selecting **Jobs** from the search drop-down list, or click **Jobs** in the menu bar. Apply more filters to narrow your search. After running a job search that yields relevant results, you can turn the **Job Alert** on to be notified when similar jobs are posted. You can also apply for jobs through LinkedIn, save and share jobs. If you come across a job better suited for one of your connections, share the job with them.

When viewing a job, see who you are connected to at that company. Sometimes a job will show the recruiter who posted it, giving you the right contact for that opportunity. Apply for the position first, then connect with the recruiter who posted the job (if that information is available) and let them know which job you applied to and how your skills are a match for that position.

MAKE JOB CONNECTIONS

After you've applied for a job, make connections with employees at that company who are in your LinkedIn network. Look for fellow veterans who work at the company, as discussed earlier using the past companies search filter and entering your branch of service.

If you find a 1st degree connection, send them a message letting them know you applied for a job at their company (be specific), and ask them how they like working there. For a 2nd degree connection, invite them to join your network, and personalize the invitation by mentioning that you applied for a job at their company. If they are a 3rd degree connection, invite them to connect with you if possible, or send them an InMail.

Remember, when connecting with someone at the company, you are not asking them to hire you or help you get the job. You are simply asking them for advice on your job search or for answers to any questions you might have about their company.

You want to build a relationship with connections and conduct informational interviews. When you build these relationships, job opportunities will often times follow.

RESEARCH YOUR CAREER

Use LinkedIn to research the skills requirements for your career field. As mentioned in the chapter on creating your profile, searching for jobs you are targeting can yield much information about the required and preferred skills. This information is helpful to see how your skills are a match for a particular job.

Also search for people on LinkedIn who have the same type of job you're pursuing. Study their profiles to see what education, certification, training, and skills they possess. This will give you a good indication of what is required for that position. Also, when studying these profiles, take note of what keywords they use to describe their skills and accomplishments. Use this information to improve your own profile.

ACCOUNT UPGRADES

LinkedIn offers account upgrades for a monthly fee. The Premium account upgrade has features that improve your LinkedIn profile's visibility, such as making you a Featured Applicant when applying for jobs through LinkedIn and appearing higher and more often in recruiters' search results. It also includes the ability to contact anyone via a set number of InMail, access to the full list of who has viewed your profile, and salary information on jobs you are interested in.

To view the Premium upgrade, visit premium.linkedin. com. Upgrades are charged automatically each month, so be sure to deactivate the upgrade on your Privacy & Settings page under the **Account** tab if you find you are no longer using the upgrade.

At the time this edition was pubished, LinkedIn was offering veterans a **free one-year Premium upgrade** to include a one-year subscription to LinkedIn Learning. To see if this is currently being offered and to request your free upgrade, visit the LinkedIn Veterans page. LinkedIn Learning is an online library of over 10,000 expert-led video courses. You can browse them from the **Learning** link found in the **Work** icon in the menu bar.

GO MOBILE

If you have a smartphone or tablet, you can use LinkedIn's various mobile apps. The LinkedIn app lets you tap into your network's updates, and it is a quick way to reach out and keep in touch with your network as well as search jobs.

There is also a Learning app and Slideshare app to let you access those platforms owned by LinkedIn. Most of the functionality you get when using LinkedIn from your computer's Internet browser is also available on the LinkedIn apps. But if you are new to LinkedIn or plan to make a lot of changes to your profile, using LinkedIn from your computer is recommended. That gives you the complete functionality and can be easier to navigate than the apps.

Once you have your profile created and have started building your network, the apps are a convenient way to keep up with your connections and conversations from anywhere. Use your time wisely while waiting in line at the grocery, for example, to check your LinkedIn app, send a few invitations, check those that are pending, and see what your connections are posting.

GET ASSISTANCE

Hopefully these chapters on LinkedIn have convinced you of its usefulness for your military-to-civilian career transition and job search. If you need assistance implementing any of the suggestions in this guide, visit LinkedIn's Help Center at help.linkedin.com or by clicking the **Me** thumbnail photo icon in the menu bar and clicking **Help** in the drop-down list. Type your question or some keywords in the search box to find answers. If you can't find the answer, scroll to the bottom of the Help Center and click **Contact us** at the bottom of the page.

Visit the LinkedIn Veterans page to access information tailored to military veterans and military spouses who are seeking jobs. For further assistance, do an Internet search to find answers to your questions. There are numerous video tutorials on the Internet that demonstrate how to use LinkedIn for your job search. Just be sure the instructions are current.

You're encouraged to explore the LinkedIn website further on your own. There is more to discover, and new items and features are constantly being added to improve this professional social networking platform.

Chapter 6

Facebook: A Different Animal

Although Facebook has some useful job search tools, it is a different animal from LinkedIn. Facebook is typically used to connect with family and friends, so the vibe is casual rather than professional.

If you have already built a network on Facebook, this chapter is for you. It describes ways to use Facebook as a positive asset to your job search. Since your network of friends and family is already established on this platform, why not use it to assist you with your job search? But it is important to be aware of the public access that your Facebook timeline may have and what it says about you.

GET NOTICED FOR THE RIGHT REASONS

Recruiters are checking your LinkedIn profile to see what you bring to the table professionally — why they should hire you. They oftentimes visit Facebook for the opposite reason — to see if there are any red flags or reasons not to hire you. Be aware that potential employers are screening your social media accounts before deciding whether to interview you and/or extend a job offer.

This doesn't mean that Facebook can't be a useful job search tool. In fact it offers valuable networking opportunities, and according to the Jobvite survey mentioned earlier, 65% of recruiters are using Facebook to showcase their employer brand, post their jobs, and vet candidates. Therefore, while you are in job search mode, it is important to review your privacy settings and check your posts and photos for their appropriateness. This goes for all your social media accounts. You want to make sure you get noticed for the right reasons!

The best approach is to keep your Facebook account clean and positive, even if you think only your friends can see it. The first part of this chapter covers adjusting the settings to control your audience and to help ensure that what others are seeing is appropriate.

NEW FACEBOOK

Facebook has recently rolled out a new look, dubbed "New Facebook," which has much of the same functionality as "Classic Facebook" but with many new changes to the look and navigation. As readers of this book could be using either the new or classic version, the following instructions and suggestions for using Facebook in your job search try to encompass both versions. Some specifics on navigating the functionality might not be as detailed if they differ greatly between versions.

REVIEW YOUR TIMELINE

Use the **View As** link to see how your timeline looks to others. To find this, go to your timeline page by clicking your name at the top of your account. Then click either the eye icon or the three horizontal dots icon to see the public's view of your timeline. Scroll through the content to see what is visible to anyone. Exit out of that view, and select **Timeline Settings** from the three dots icon to review your Timeline and Tagging Settings and adjust them as appropriate.

REVIEW YOUR ACTIVITY

Also from your timeline page, click **Activity Log** (three dots icon) to view your posts and tagged activity. Click on each of the links for Timeline Review, Tag Review, and Photo Review to see if anything requires your attention.

On the Activity Log, review your posts, the activity you're tagged in, and photos and videos (you might have to click the **Filter** link to select and view each of these). Remove or untag yourself from posts as needed by clicking either the the three dots icon or pencil icon next to the post, and then clicking **Delete** if it is your post or **Remove Tag** if it is someone else's post.

SET THE AUDIENCE OF POSTS

Change the audience of your posts that need adjusting as appropriate. In the Activity Log, click on a post on the left, and then edit the audience either by clicking the down arrow next to the audience icon or by clicking the three dots icon. Select the appropriate audience from the list. Your audience choices are Public, Friends, Friends except, Specific friends, Only Me, or selecting from your lists, such as Close Friends (lists are explained later).

When posting on your home page, you control the audience of new posts the same as above. Before clicking the **Post** button, select who can view the post from the audience drop-down list.

Limit the audience of old posts from your privacy settings. Click the triangle in the upper right corner, select **Settings & Privacy** or **Settings** from the drop-down list, then click **Privacy** on the left. Click **Limit Past Posts** on the right. Content on your timeline you have shared with friends-of-friends or public will change to friends only. Be selective when accepting friend requests, since they have the most visibility to your activity.

SET YOUR NOTIFICATIONS

You can adjust the activity notifications you receive from Facebook on your **Settings** page. Click the **Notifications** link and review all the options to choose what you are notified about and how you get the notifications. The types of notifications vary depending on if you are using a desktop or mobile device, so explore all your options.

BEEF UP YOUR PROFILE

Update your profile to include your professional side, especially if you plan to use Facebook's job search capability. You may not have been thinking in those terms when you created your account. Including in your profile the keywords and phrases that describe your skills will help Facebook's Jobs functionality work better in matching you to relevant jobs and companies. It will also help convey your skills to your network of friends who might assist with your job search. Update your profile from the **Edit Profile** link on your timeline page.

Facebook profile pictures tend to be casual. However, while you are in job search mode, it is best to use the same professional-looking photo across all your social media accounts. This gives you a consistent professional presence online. Also add a cover photo to your Facebook profile, similar to LinkedIn's background image. This should be something that reflects your industry or professional interests to help boost your professional branding.

Include a Bio, similar to your LinkedIn headline, and complete the About Info. You could use your LinkedIn summary for the Details About You section. Also complete the Work and Education sections.

When editing your profile sections, the audience icon will be visible. Click the icon and select from the list the appropriate audience for that section of your profile.

CREATE A LIST FOR YOUR JOB SEARCH

Facebook gives you the ability to organize your friends network into lists. This is especially helpful if your network is large. The lists feature allows you to see updates from a specific group or to post an update to specific people.

To access lists, click **Friend Lists** in the list on the left side of your home page (click the See More link if Friend Lists is not visible). Facebook creates the default lists of Acquaintances, Close Friends, and Restricted, and allows you to create your own custom lists.

Create a custom list called "Job Search" for friends who are involved in your transition or those who could help with your job search. To create a custom list, click **+ Create List**, then name the list, and add appropriate friends to it. When you click this list in the future, it will allow you to see what those friends are posting without being distracted by everyone else's posts. This helps you focus your time spent on Facebook for your job search.

The list feature also lets you share your posts to a specific audience. Your custom "Job Search" list will show in the drop-down list of the audience selector, letting you choose that list and share your post with only that group.

SEARCH FOR JOBS

You can find jobs on Facebook by clicking the **Jobs** or **Hiring** link (look for the briefcase icon) in the list to the left of your home page (click See More to expand the list). Jobs may also be viewed from a company's business page if there is a **Jobs** link on their page.

To search for jobs, click the **Jobs** link from your home page. Enter keywords in the job search box, and select options for job type and category. The default location is set to your current geographic area, but you can change this by clicking the **Change** link next to it.

Scroll through the returned jobs, and click on a job title to view the full description. You can apply to a job on Facebook by clicking the **Apply Now** button. It will auto-populate your information (which you can edit) and prompt you to answer questions the employer included. Your application will be sent as a message to the employer, and you can then communicate with them via Messenger.

You can also save the job to view later and share the job with others in your network. While searching jobs, you can turn on notifications of newly posted jobs in your area by clicking the **Subscribe** button.

RESEARCH COMPANIES

Use the Facebook search box to find a company you are interested in, and visit the company's page. Scroll through the company's posts to see what information and updates they are sharing. Often their posts will show you what is happening at the company and what the culture is like. They might also include details about their hiring efforts or career opportunities.

Learn more about the company by exploring the links on their page, which could include About, Jobs, Photos, Videos, or Events. Also click the **Like** or **Follow** button to be a fan and have their updates show up in your news feed. Seeing what companies are posting about can be a valuable research tool for your job search.

JOIN GROUPS

You can join groups on Facebook to connect with people who share similar interests. More emphasis is put on the groups functionality in the "New" Facebook version, and there will be a groups icon at the top of your account. Explore groups to expand your network, just as you were encouraged to do in the LinkedIn chapter on networking.

GET THE WORD OUT

Let your Facebook network of friends and family know you are transitioning and searching for a civilian job. Post positive status updates about your job search. Your family and friends have a vested interest in helping you succeed, and you never know when an aunt, cousin, or old friend may come up with a job opportunity for you.

Should you decide to keep your Facebook out of your job search, be sure your privacy settings are properly adjusted, as mentioned earlier. Set them so your timeline can be viewed by friends only.

GET ASSISTANCE

As with most social media platforms, Facebook has a help center where you can find answers to your questions. For assistance, click the triangle at the top right of your account and click **Help & Support**, or click the question mark at the top right and click the **Help Center** link. You can also find helpful information about using Facebook by searching the Internet.

Chapter 7

Twitter: A Surprisingly Useful Job Search Tool

Twitter is a surprisingly beneficial tool to help you get noticed, get connected, and get opportunities -- which, as stated in chapter one, are the three main reasons to use social media in your job search. Users post "tweets" up to 280 characters long, much like texting, keeping the messages short and sweet.

How can this type of social media platform be useful to your job search? When used strategically, Twitter offers a wealth of industry knowledge. It can also help establish your professional online presence, showing your expertise and passion for your industry.

This chapter gives you suggestions for using Twitter effectively for your job search. Give it a try and you might be surprised by its usefulness.

GET NOTICED

Unlike with LinkedIn, where you should have only one account/one profile, on Twitter you can have multiple accounts and designate one of them for your professional side. Other accounts can be used for your hobbies or connecting with friends. Your professional Twitter account should reflect the industry and jobs you are targeting. Although a Twitter profile is much simpler than a LinkedIn or Facebook profile, it still contains useful information about you. Here are some tips for building your professional Twitter profile:

USE YOUR REAL NAME

Use your real name on your profile and handle to help with name recognition. If your name is taken, you could add a designation matching your profession, like @John-SmithPMP. But keep it as short as possible. That way it won't take up too many of the 280 characters when your handle is mentioned in someone else's tweet or when your content is retweeted.

ADD A PHOTO

Add a profile photo to increase the personal connection between you and those viewing your Twitter account. Use a photo that is professional and friendly. Again, keep your profile photo consistent across your social media accounts while you are in job search mode. You can spruce up your account more by adding a header photo.

A good rule while in job search mode is to keep the elements of your Twitter profile simple, but this all depends on the type of job you are targeting. A program manager or defense contractor may want a simple, clean header photo, while someone looking for a job in graphic design could get creative with their Twitter header to show off their artistic talent.

INCLUDE YOUR LOCATION AND WEBSITE

You can include your location in your profile if it is relevant to the job you are seeking. Include a website where employers can get more information about you, like the link to your Linkedin profile or other social media channels.

USE KEYWORDS

Load your bio with keywords. Your Twitter bio is like your LinkedIn headline — it tells what you bring to the table in 160 characters. Load it with keywords describing your skills and expertise to make each character count. Use your LinkedIn headline plus a few additional keywords.

ADJUST YOUR SETTINGS

Twitter is a public network, and depending on your profile settings, everything you tweet could be sent out to the twittersphere. Take a moment to adjust your settings such as Account, Security and privacy, and Notifications. Read through all of the options to select the settings that work best for you. To get to your settings, click **More** to the left, then click **Settings and privacy** from the drop-down list. Check your options for **Privacy and safety**.

You can add your mobile phone number in the **Notifications** settings to use Twitter's SMS notifications functionality. Under **Preferences**, click the **SMS notifications** link. Add your phone number, and check the box next to **Tweets**. This will send you notifications of people you follow if you enable it from their accounts, which is described later. Set other notifications, such as when someone retweets your content or mentions you, to be alerted and reminded to check your Twitter account.

TWEET YOUR MESSAGE

Tweeting is a way to get noticed and share information on Twitter. You don't have to tweet in order to use Twitter as a job search tool, but posting tweets will help you build your network and online presence. The more tweets you post, the more people will notice and follow you on Twitter. And the more followers you have, the more exposure you will receive.

What should you tweet? Since you're limited to 280 characters per tweet, you are forced to keep it concise. Share interesting and relevant content, such as a link to an article in your industry, advice and expertise, or a positive comment about your job search. Remind your followers that you are in job search mode, and let them know about your career goals.

ENGAGE WITH EXPERTS

Twitter is not just for broadcasting and collecting information, you can also use it for conversing. Engage with experts in your industry and with companies of interest to help build your network and get noticed. You can engage with others on Twitter by mentioning them in a tweet, replying to or retweeting what they've posted, or getting involved in Twitter chats.

MENTION A USERNAME

By mentioning another Twitter user in your tweets, you will catch their attention and can start a conversation with them. Mention them by including @username anywhere in the tweet. If you begin a tweet with @username, it will be treated like a reply to that user. So if you do not intend it as a reply, add a period before the @ symbol. Mentions will show up on the Notifications page.

RETWEET & REPLY

Retweeting is sharing someone else's tweet that you found relevant. Click the **Retweet** icon (square of arrows) below a tweet to share that person's tweet with your followers. The person will know that you have retweeted them, and they will most likely be appreciative and pleased that you found their post interesting. This is a great way to get on someone's radar, like a recruiter, for instance.

You can also reply to a tweet to make the conversation personal by clicking the chat bubble icon below the tweet. A reply begins with @username and shows up in the recipient's Notifications. When a tweet starts with @ username, only the sender and recipient and those who follow both will see it in their timeline.

PARTICIPATE IN TWITTER CHATS

Twitter chats, also called tweet chats, are virtual conversations linked by a common hashtag (#). A group of people tweet about a subject of interest using #chatname in their tweets to link them together. Participating in these online conversations offers excellent opportunities to learn about industry topics, network with others who share a similar interest, and showcase your expertise.

Formal Twitter chats are arranged in advance to occur at a certain time, usually scheduled every week or month. They often have a moderator and speakers taking part. For example, the #JobHuntChat occurs every Monday at 9 PM (ET), where job seekers ask questions, compare experiences, and get advice from each other and career experts.

To find a tweet chat relevant to your industry, interests, or job search, do an Internet search on keywords "tweet chat" plus your topic of interest. To follow or join the chat, type #chatname in the Twitter search box to see the tweets linked by the hashtag. You can also track chats and trending topics using a social media aggregator, as described in a later chapter.

GET CONNECTED

Use Twitter to follow and connect with people that can help with your job search and give you valuable industry content. It is a remarkable resource for connecting with other like-minded people tweeting about the things you are interested in. You can see what others (and companies) are talking about and what is relevant to them.

To follow a Twitter account, first click their name to bring up their bio and a list of their most recent tweets. If these look relevant to you, click the **Follow** button. Now their tweets will appear in your timeline.

SEARCH WITH HASHTAGS

The purpose of including a hashtag (#) before a word or phrase is to label and categorize the tweet, which will make it show up in a search. Type an industry keyword or trending topic, for example, into the Twitter search box and the resulting list of tweets will contain that word or phrase and possibly other hashtags to further your search. Clicking on a hashtag brings up other tweets marked with the same word or phrase.

Searching for keywords, such as #jobsearch, #careertips, and keywords in your industry, will help you find accounts to follow. There are many Twitter accounts that tweet job search advice and tips, such as @CorporateGray. You can also find career coaches and industry experts to follow. Search on companies you are targeting to find not only the company's main account, but also the company's "careers" account. They may have an account called @CompanyJobs, for example, that posts their jobs and information about their hiring process.

There are third-party tools, such as TweetDeck and Hootsuite, that allow you to track tweets based on hashtags and search terms. These useful social media aggregators are described in a later chapter. Although hashtags originated with Twitter, they are now being used widely on other social media platforms as well.

ORGANIZE WITH LISTS

A Twitter list is an organized group of Twitter users, similar to the lists on Facebook. You can create your own lists or subscribe to lists created by others. Viewing a list's timeline will show you the tweets from only those users on the list. As with Facebook, using lists helps you filter out the "noise" to focus on what just those accounts are posting.

Get to your lists page by clicking **Lists** to the left of your account. You'll see the lists you've created or subscribed to. Click the "more" three horizontal dots icon to see the lists you are on.

To create a new list, click the **Create list** plus sign icon. Add a title, like "Job Search," and description, then add the Twitter user accounts that will make up the list. You don't have to be following a user to add them to your list. Create a list for your industry or job search to keep track of relevant Twitter users.

See the lists of others by going to their Twitter profile. Click the "more" three horizontal dots icon at the top of their page and click **View Lists** from the drop-down to see what lists they have created or subscribed to. Click the list name to see tweets of the members. If a list looks relevant, add it to your account by clicking the **Subscribe** or **Follow** button. Also, follow any relevant members that you discover in the lists.

GET OPPORTUNITIES

Following recruiters, companies, and job listing accounts will bring opportunities to your Twitter timeline. You'll see what companies and recruiters are posting and what jobs are available.

There are Twitter accounts that exist solely for the purpose of tweeting job postings as soon as they open.

Now there is a great resource for your job search, and probably the best way to use Twitter's fast-paced system of information sharing.

How do you find these job listing accounts to follow? Use the search box and enter keywords specific to the job or industry you are targeting (#finance, #salesjobs), your location (#chicagojobs, #dcjobs), company names, or general job listings (#jobs, #hiring).

BE MOBILE

Because Twitter moves so quickly (thousands of tweets a second and millions a day), tweets will become buried if you don't check your Twitter timeline often. There are a few ways to make sure you don't miss important tweets. This is where mobile notifications comes into play.

Remember adding your phone number to your settings? When you find a relevant account to follow and you do not want to miss any of their tweets, you can activate the SMS Notifications for that Twitter account. Go to their profile page by clicking their name, then click the bell with plus sign icon next to the Following button to turn on notifications to your mobile phone.

Use this feature for accounts you want instant notification of, like a job listing account, so you'll be texted about the job as soon as it is tweeted. However, be discriminating about turning on mobile notifications for accounts you are following. If you activate too many of these, your phone will be receiving texts constantly and it will become noise instead of useful and timely information.

Another way to keep track of tweets on the go is to download the Twitter app to your phone. This lets you join the conversation from anywhere. From the app you'll have access to your timeline, notifications, and mentions.

GET ASSISTANCE

As with the other social media sites mentioned thus far, you can find answers and assistance from the platform's help center. To get help from Twitter, click the **More** link to the left of your account, and select **Help Center** from the drop-down list. You can also go to support.twitter. com. or search for your answer on the Internet.

Are you convinced that Twitter can be useful to your job search? Just simply following relevant accounts will bring you a wealth of information about any topic. But try joining the conversation and you'll see how valuable and supportive this community can be.

Chapter 8

Think SEO

Creating an online professional presence will make you searchable on the Internet by your skills and expertise. Why is this important? When your resume comes across a hiring manager's desk, one of the first things they will do is run an Internet search on you to see what comes up. If you have a LinkedIn profile and other professional references online, those will come up high in the results.

Google is referenced throughout this chapter because it is currently the largest and most popular Internet search engine. However, most of ideas covered in this chapter could apply to many of the other Internet search engines. But for simplicity's sake, let's just use Google here.

SEARCH ENGINE OPTIMIZATION

Following the advice already mentioned in this book can increase your search engine optimization, or SEO, by leaps and bounds. But what does that mean?

SEO is the methodology used to obtain a high-ranking placement in Internet search engine results. If you "Google" yourself, you will see what comes up when someone (like a recruiter, for example) searches for you online. Having a complete LinkedIn profile, and sharing interesting and meaningful content online, will increase your online presence and put it nearer the top of someone's search results. That's the definition and goal of SEO.

Build your online presence and be seen as an industry leader by sharing your expertise, thoughts on current industry topics, and links to relevant articles. Sharing valuable and relevant content boosts your SEO value.

SEARCHING 101

While recruiters are running searches on candidates (like you), job seekers should be running their own searches to help with their career transition. Recruiters are typically adept at online searching because it is oftentimes part of their job. But this might be something new to you as a job seeker.

There are basic rules for searching on Google that can also apply across most search engines. Some of these rules to keep in mind are as follows.

Google assumes an "and" between the words you enter in your search. So searching on: *logistics jobs Chicago* is the same as using "and" between each word, and it will show you results that have those three terms scattered throughout the content.

If you want the words found together, use quotations around them to indicate that they are a string, like *"program manager" jobs*. This will search content containing the words program manager together and the word jobs.

Upper and lowercase letters are ignored except when using "or." Put the OR in all caps and separate the "or" terms from the rest with parenthesis. For example, *logistics jobs (Chicago OR Detroit)* will return content containing the words logistics and jobs, plus either Chicago or Detroit.

Use the minus sign to exclude words from the search. For example, *logistics jobs -Chicago* will return content that includes logistics and jobs but excludes the content that also contains Chicago.

You can search for content on a specific website by including *site:* in your search terms. For example, *logistics jobs site:linkedin.com* will search for content containing logistics and jobs on LinkedIn.com without having to login to your LinkedIn account.

LEVERAGE ADVANCED CAPABILITIES

There are advanced tools on Google that you can leverage for your job search. Google (or any similar Internet search engine) can be a valuable resource for researching companies, job opportunities, career fields, people, and more.

You can focus your search results by choosing the category of your search. Rather than running a default search on all categories, choose a specific content category by clicking the appropriate term near the top of the search results page. Choose from news, images, videos, and more.

Google lets you search the results from a specific time frame in the past. This is helpful in filtering your search by current results. To set the time frame, click **Tools** at the top of search results, then click the **Any time** link. Choose a time frame from the drop-down list or set a custom range.

GOOGLE ALERTS

Google also provides tools to help you keep track of your interests online without having to run the searches daily. You can set-up alerts to receive web content on industry news, companies you are targeting, job opportunities, colleagues, influencers, and your own online reputation.

First run the search to test how well your search criteria filter the content you want to monitor. Make your terms specific and precise to focus the content and ensure it will be relevant. Using terms that are too generic or common will not return useful information.

Once you decide on the keywords that return useful content, go to google.com/alerts, and make sure you are logged in to the Google account you want to use. Enter your keywords and set the frequency for receiving the alerts. Also choose the category to track, like news, blogs, videos, etc. and the region. Once you set-up an alert, the latest content will be sent to you via email.

Set-up an alert to monitor your own Internet presence by using your name as the search terms. You'll be notified if new content is shared on the Internet that contains your name. These Google alerts do not search social media sites, so this is not a substitute for monitoring your presence on LinkedIn and other social media platforms you are using.

GET ASSISTANCE

There is additional hidden potential for your job search offered by Internet search engines. Learn more about using Google from the help center at support.google.com. Find answers to many of the questions you might have as you explore the search engine to make it work harder for you.

There is also a wealth of information that can be found from forums, instructional videos, advice articles, and more that will answer your questions about anything and everything. "Google it" to find answers, whether it is help with your job search or to find information that can further your career goals.

The case for having an online professional presence is strong when you consider the power of SEO and the wide use of Internet search engines. Creating your professional profile online, posting valuable content on social media, and building your relevant network will all yield results for your job search.

Chapter 9

Visual Networks

Visual content is important in this day and age, and there are popular social media platforms that focus on visual content. Having a presence on these networks can be useful in your career transition. This chapter covers some of these that you should consider using to help you get noticed, build your network, and find opportunities. You may already have an account with some of these, so read on to learn ways of using them in your job search that you may not have thought of.

LIGHTS, CAMERA, ACTION

Ever wanted to star in your own video? If this interests you, consider creating and posting a video resume to YouTube or Vimeo. Both these platforms will allow you to create a free account, or channel, and upload your videos to it. You could create a video resume for your job search, or create other types of videos that show your expertise.

Video resumes have gained in popularity recently. They allow you to show your expertise and background in a more interesting and visual format.

What recruiter wouldn't prefer watching a short video of you talking about your expertise, rather than reading your written resume? Not that your resume isn't riveting, but a short and captivating video can be much more memorable.

You just need to make sure it is memorable in a good way -- showing your professionalism and passion for your industry. Here are some tips to keep in mind when creating your video resume:

- Keep the video short and to the point
- Describe the value you bring to a certain position
- Explain why you're the best person for the job
- Talk about your background and experience
- Make it professional looking, upbeat, and engaging
- Let your passion for the industry shine through

Get ideas for creating your video resume by searching YouTube, Vimeo, and the Internet for examples. You will find both good and bad examples to learn from. There are companies that will create your video resume for you. It does not have to be a professionally produced product, but it should show you looking and sounding professional. You can also design your channel and profile to make them reflect your professionalism.

When uploading your video, add a catchy, relevant title and plenty of keywords in the description that reflect your skills and expertise. After you upload it, the video will have a URL that you can share with recruiters, add to your resume, and include on your other social media accounts. Remember that you can add web links to your LinkedIn profile, so share your video by adding the link to the featured section of your LinkedIn profile.

INSTAGRAM - PROFESSIONAL BRANDING

Instagram's popularity is proof of the importance of visual content and networking in today's social media arena. It is a huge network of users from all industries, so it can be a great platform to tap into for your job search.

Instagram is a mobile application that allows you to create, edit, caption, and share your photos and videos. It has built-in editing features, and your photos and videos can be easily shared on multiple social media sites at once. It also has features for recording and sharing your stories and live videos (IGTV). If you have work-related photos and videos to share, this is a good place to broaden your reach and increase your online presence.

If you are currently using Instagram for your personal photos, create a separate account for sharing your professional images. Similar to Twitter, you can have multiple accounts that serve different purposes (hobbies and friends vs. business and colleagues).

As with the other social profiles used for your job search, make sure your professional Instagram account's username and bio consistently reflect your professionalism and strengths. You can also add a link in your profile, such as to your LinkedIn public profile or to your video resume.

Share photos on Instagram that show the type of work you do, like images of your artwork, designs, and projects, if applicable to your industry. If you are not in a visual or creative industry, you could post photos and videos of you demonstrating a particular skill or talking about a project you are working on. Or post photos of you at work and attending professional conferences and industry-related events. Of course, only post work photos, videos, and information about projects that you are allowed to share.

Search for and follow relevant Instagram accounts, such as companies and industry experts, to build your network. Like and comment on users' photos to get on their radar. Use industry-related hashtags in captions and comments to network with others in your field. Hashtags are used abundantly on Instagram, so be liberal in adding relevant tags to what you share.

PIN YOUR INTERESTS

According to its website, Pinterest is a "tool for collecting and organizing things you love." It lets you pin and organize images from a website or upload images from your computer or phone.

How can pinning and organizing images and visual content be a useful job search tool? An obvious answer would be to display your portfolio if you are in a visual industry, such as interior or graphic design. Pinning images of your work is a way to showcase your talent.

But you don't have to be in a visual industry to benefit from using Pinterest. You can show your interests and expertise by pinning links to articles you've been quoted in or have written, relevant articles that show your interest in your career field, professional organizations of which you are a member, and of course, your resume.

Use captions to describe your pins, and include keywords and phrases for the industry or skills they show. These keywords, or tags, will make your pins more likely to show in a search.

A Pinterest board is how you organize your pins. You can have a resume board where you pin the different parts of your resume. Each pin can highlight a different section of your resume. Create an industry or current events board to show your interests and experience. If your work is visual, create a board with samples of your best pieces, or a board of others' work that you admire.

Follow industry leaders to learn what is trending in your career field. Repinning relevant posts is similar to retweeting on Twitter and is often appreciated by the original pinner.

You won't just find recipe, home improvement, and fashion inspiration on Pinterest (although searching on what to wear for an interview can be helpful). Search for samples of resumes on Pinterest to get ideas for improving your own. You'll also find a plethora of job search advice being pinned.

The goal of sharing things on Pinterest is to get them shared, so make sure things you pin are interesting and inspiring. Keep your public boards positive and professional.

Chapter 10

But Wait, There's More...

There are many more social media-related job search tools available online, and this book does not cover them all. But a few more tools are worth mentioning, as these can help you build and manage your professional online presence and stay connected to a supportive network.

BLOG ABOUT YOUR PASSION

Having your own blog is an excellent way to build a professional presence on the Internet and establish yourself as an expert in your industry. Blogging is not for everyone, as it requires prolific writing. If you are passionate about your work and you love to write, then consider creating your own blog.

There are numerous free blog platforms that let you set up your own blog quickly, such as Wix, Joomla, or Wordpress, just to name a few. If writing is your strength and you have a lot to say about your profession, having a blog can be a real asset in your quest for employment.

Your blog will have a URL that you can share with recruiters, include on your resume, and add to your LinkedIn profile and other social media profiles. You can also link your blog to your social media accounts to direct readers to your online network. Set up your blog to accept comments from readers to encourage conversations on the topics you write about.

An extra advantage to having a blog is that it will appear high in the results of a search engine (SEO again!), should a recruiter be looking for you on the Internet. It's another way to have a professional online presence that shows your expertise.

Not interested in having your own blog but still have expertise to share? You can publish your articles on LinkedIn, as mentioned earlier. Another option is to offer to be a guest author for blogs that have good visibility within your industry. Submit your ideas for articles to the blog managers, and let them know you are willing to share relevant, insightful content with their readers. After your article has been published on a site, attach that link to your LinkedIn profile and share it on all your social media channels.

MEETUP IN PERSON

For those interested in networking face-to-face, Meetup (www.meetup.com) is a social media site that allows groups to organize and gather in local communities with the goal of improving themselves or their community. You can search for organized groups by topic and within a certain radius of your location.

Look for job search support groups that might be meeting in your community. Often these groups invite guest speakers to join their meet up and assist group members with resume writing, give job search advice, and help connect you with recruiters. The scheduled meet ups take place in person, although group members can comment and interact online as well.

Search Meetup for business networking groups in your industry, or for any local groups in which you share an interest, like a hobby or volunteer cause. Networking does not have to be just about business.

Reach out to Meetup organizers from the group's home page. Group organizers are often well-connected and can help you get introduced to appropriate people. Attend events to form valuable relationships with group organizers and members.

MANAGE YOUR ACCOUNTS

There are so many social media sites to help with your job search, how will you keep them all straight? If you have multiple social media accounts, you can manage them more efficiently by using a third-party aggregator to consolidate them into one place. Social media management tools help you manage your content and networks across multiple platforms from one site. There are numerous applications to choose from, such as Hootsuite, Buffer, or Sprout Social.

Some of these allow you to set up columns (or streams, as they're called on Hootsuite) to track posts based on search terms. This helps you track topics of interest across your social channels. You can also set up a stream to track relevant groups and companies, which helps you stay focused and block out the noise when you are checking on each of your accounts. Or set up a stream to track your mentions.

Some aggregators will let you schedule your posts, so you can create the content when it is convenient, and then control the day and time it will be posted. This is useful if you are using social media late at night or early in the morning, but you want the content posted at a time when more people are likely to see it. The ability to schedule your content is a great reason to use a social media management tool, even if you only have one social media account to manage.

GOOGLE YOURSELF

As mentioned in the chapter on SEO, and worth mentioning again, you should regularly search for yourself on the Internet to keep tabs on your online presence, or your digital footprint. When a company recruiter does an Internet search on your name, what do they see? Google yourself to make sure that what is coming up shows your professional online presence. Things that are likely to be returned near the top would be your LinkedIn and other social media profiles, your blog or articles you have written online, or your video resume.

Be sure to set up a Google Alert described earlier to help you keep tabs on your online presence. Have it search your name and location and notify you when there is new content on the Internet that includes those terms.

GENERATE A QR CODE

QR codes are two dimensional barcodes that store information in a visual pattern. Unlike a one dimensional barcode that stores 20-25 characters, a QR code can store up to 2,000 characters.

QR codes typically store a website URL, but they can also be used to store contact information or even a personal summary.

Do an Internet search on QR code generators to find websites that allow you to generate your own QR code image. This code could contain your contact information or the link to one of your social media accounts, like your LinkedIn profile or your blog. You can download the QR code image and add it to your resume, email signature, or transition business card to give recruiters more information about you.

Be sure to test the QR code you generate before sharing it to make sure it contains the correct information. A

QR code reader app on a smartphone will scan the code. It is recommended you use an app that scans the code and displays the information it contains, rather than one that scans and opens the link automatically. You want to check the link first before you open it.

CONNECT WITH FELLOW VETERANS

There are military veterans in every civilian industry, and they have been through the transition that you are making now from the military-to-civilian workplace. They can be a powerful network, bringing a wealth of knowledge and support for your job search.

Social media platforms are a great way to find veterans in your industry or at a company you are targeting. Search for them on social media and connect with them. You can ask them for advice and perform informational interviews. As mentioned earlier, you are not asking those you connect with for a job, simply for information, advice, and to keep you in mind for future opportunities.

There are also websites that allow you to search for fellow veterans by industry, branch of service, rank when they left the military, and more. The Buddy Finder at www.military.com/buddy-finder, is one such resource to help you find and connect with veterans working in companies, government agencies, industries, or locations that you are targeting for your job search. Another veteran database is VetFriends.com. You can sign up for a free membership to these sites and then have access to their network of veterans.

Chapter 11

Balance and Beyond

Finding a balance between using these social media tools, applying the traditional job search methods, and all while still working full-time at your active-duty position can be tricky. Take it one step at a time, adjusting your priorities as you go. The time and effort you devote toward building your online professional presence and your social media networks now can go a long way toward landing your next job and beyond.

SUPPLEMENT THE TRADITIONAL TOOLS

Don't disregard the traditional job search methods you learn about in the military's Transition GPS class. They are important components of your job search. You should still create a resume and cover letters, attend job fairs and in-person networking events, make phone calls, and request face-to-face informational interviews.

Social media does not replace these traditional tools, it supplements them to make your job search more effective. You have learned how it can help you to get noticed for your expertise, make broader but relevant connections, research your industry, and find companies and job opportunities you may not have learned about otherwise. This book described numerous ways social media can give you an extra advantage and expand your job search.

DEDICATE A FEW MINUTES A DAY

You are currently extremely busy juggling your active-duty job and your transition at the same time. A job search is time consuming enough without adding more than the traditional tools to the chore. How can you make time and put to good use what you have learned about these social media tools?

Pick and choose the tools that feel right for you, and budget the time spent on your social media accounts. If you only have time to focus on one, choose LinkedIn, as this is the largest professional network and the one recruiters use the most. Or, if you have already established a presence and large network on Facebook, for example, then maybe that is the platform you should leverage most for your job search.

The time you spend initially setting up a complete and effective professional profile will be well worth it. Then you can dedicate just 15-20 minutes a day for the purpose of making new connections, posting relevant content, contributing to group discussions, or researching jobs and companies. There is plenty to be done, but it does not all have to be done in each sitting.

Don't get sucked into the black hole of trolling the social media site without a purpose. That is a time drainer that you cannot afford. Instead, focus your efforts when you go online. The bulk of your time spent on social media should be in sharing your strengths and experience and in making meaningful connections.

Social media is not a quick fix for your job search. It takes time to establish your online presence and build a meaningful and supportive network. You have to be willing to invest the effort necessary to nurture relationships you make online and show yourself as an expert in your field.

GIVE BACK & PAY IT FORWARD

Show interest in what others say and reciprocate any support you receive. The job search tips throughout this guide have focused on how to show-off your skills and strengths, but your use of social media should not be all about self-promotion.

Share jobs you're not suited for with other connections that might be interested. Engage with others and offer advice and information to those with whom you connect. You will gain more from meaningful interactions and spreading good vibes throughout your networks than from just looking out for your own interests.

And once you are securely ensconced in your civilian job, reach out to other transitioning military members to support their job search. Share your story with them and offer advice from your transition experience. Let them know what worked for you and be honest about what did not work, so others can learn from your mistakes. Help them get connected to the right people in their industry. Pay forward the support you receive during your transition and job search.

KEEP EXPLORING

This book was meant to give you a reference for current popular social media platforms and online job search tools, and show you how to best use them to increase the effectiveness of your job search. The more popular the site, the more possible connections and opportunities it can offer.

However, there are many more platforms and online tools out there, and new ones are constantly being created and can rapidly gain in popularity. Explore the Internet further for tools appropriate for your own transition and job search.

DON'T SET IT AND FORGET IT

Once you have built your online professional profile, don't sit back and relax, expecting the job offers to start rolling in. It takes regular attention to stay active and noticed on social media. Even if it is just 15 minutes a day spent checking your updates, or posting content, or connecting with others. A regular level of activity will keep your presence building, improving, and working for your job search.

And most of these online networking tools will prove valuable beyond your job search. An investment in building your professional online presence and network now will continue to benefit you throughout your civilian career.

After your transition, continue to actively build your network of colleagues in your industry and participate on the social media channels where you have established a presence. You will continue to learn and grow in your career and will keep yourself open to new opportunities, even when you are not looking for them.

Good luck with your military-to-civilian transition, and thank you for your service to our country!

Websites

The following websites were referenced in this book:

Buffer.com
CorporateGray.com
Facebook.com
Google.com
Hootsuite.com
Instagram.com
Jobvite.com
Joomla.com
LinkedIn.com
Meetup.com
Military.com/buddy-finder
Pinterest.com
SproutSocial.com
Tweetdeck.twitter.com
Twitter.com
VetFriends.com
Vimeo.com
Wix.com
Wordpress.com
YouTube.com

Help Centers

Use the help centers below for assistance with these social media platforms:

- Facebook: www.facebook.com/help
- Google: https://support.google.com
- Linkedin: http://help.linkedin.com
- Twitter: http://support.twitter.com

Also, as mentioned earlier, searching the Internet can help you find answers to your social media questions. You'll find numerous articles, forums, and video tutorials that demonstrate how to use the different social media platforms. Be sure the instructions you refer to are current, as these sites are constantly changing their features and functionality.

Corporate Gray's 9-Step Transition Process

The focus of this book has been on helping transitioning military members and veterans with their job search, so including a useful synopsis of The Nine-Step Military Transition Process seemed appropriate. This is a step-by-step approach to the military-to-civilian career transition, helping you clarify your goals, get moving in the right direction, save time and effort, minimize your costs, and connect with an excellent first post-service job.

Outlined here are the overall concepts from Corporate Gray's *Military-to-Civilian Transition Guide* to help you make a successful career transition. The full print version, with more than 4 million copies in distribution, remains the most widely used transition guide for military members, veterans, and their families. These steps can also be accessed online at www.CorporateGray.com.

1. DEVELOP YOUR TRANSITION PLAN

As with any military operation, it is important to establish a timeline and be disciplined in the execution of your planned activities. Developing a sound yet flexible job search plan is critical to conducting a successful employment campaign. The time spent planning and organizing your activities will result in a far more effective job search.

The job market is in a constant state of change. Individuals with the right education, skills, and experience are in a better position to find good jobs that should lead to career advancement in the years ahead. Research careers using social media as described in this book. Also check out the list of the fastest growing occupations to the year 2028 found on the U.S. Department of Labor's Occupational Outlook Handbook at www.bls.gov/ooh.

2. OBTAIN TRANSITION ASSISTANCE

There are many organizations that assist the military job seeker with their transition to the civilian workplace.

The military's Transition GPS Program provides core services including skills assessment, resume writing, interviewing skills, salary negotiations, dressing for success, and more.

Federal and state agencies sponsor high quality transition services. A list of free resources and websites to assist with your transition and job search can be found in Step 2 of the online Transition Guide at CorporateGray.com.

There are also many civilian websites offering free resources to help with your transition. Search the Internet on "military transition" to find a wealth of assistance online.

3. BUILD YOUR NETWORK

Networking in the job search involves connecting and interacting with people who can be helpful to you. There are many resources to assist you in identifying and extending your network through new associations and organizations.

After reading this social media book, you now know how to find and connect with individuals by using your social media channels. You've seen how this will grow your network exponentially. Another avenue to build your professional network is joining and participating in professional associations, of which there are many for military service members. Join organizations in your community, such as the Rotary Club, Lions Club, and faith-based organizations, to build your local network.

Keep information about your networking contacts organized. Collect business cards at networking events and follow-up with individuals to build valuable relationships.

4. ASSESS YOUR SKILLS & INTERESTS

To best position yourself in the job market, you should pay particular attention to identifying and refining your present skills and achieving new and more marketable skills.

Take stock of what skills you possess from your military service. Include both your work-content (hard) skills and functional (soft) skills. Then research what skills you will need for pursuing a civilian career. You can identify civilian credentialing requirements using these resources:

www.cool.osd.mil/army

www.cool.navy.mil

www.careeronestop.org/Credentials

Assess your skills and interests through testing and assessment instruments used by many career counselors. The Strong Interest Inventory and the Myers-Briggs Assessment are two tools for assessing career interests which are accessible through the DoL/VETS transition assistance program. The O*Net Interest Profiler, found at www.mynextmove.org/explore/ip, is another useful tool to help you explore your work and personal interests.

If your self-assessment activities indicate that your abilities and skills are entrepreneurial, you may be best suited for self-employment. Many of the skills and personal qualities you may have acquired while in the service are well suited for becoming a successful entrepreneur.

5. USE YOUR EDUCATION BENEFITS

Many transitioning military have the advantage of great educational benefits - especially the Post-9/11 GI Bill. Advanced education or additional training can make you more competitive in the job market and can also pay off down the road in earnings.

Consider thinking outside the box. Look at all possibilities – public universities, private colleges, training and certification programs. A workshop or a seminar can be effective without being time-consuming. Be sure to pursue training that aligns well with your industry and will give you a leg up when employers are comparing you to other candidates.

Depending on your circumstances, evaluate whether a local or online program, as well as a part-time or full-time basis is best suited to your needs. There are many online degree programs that allow you to pursue your education remotely. Also, many schools offer credit for your military experience.

Put your future on track for success and boost your job and earning opportunities by using your military education benefits, and never stop learning.

6. CONSTRUCT YOUR RESUME

Resumes are important tools for communicating your purpose and capabilities to employers. You can craft your resume by understanding resume types, construction elements, and the refinements necessary to make it your effective first impression to employers. Read about these in Step 6 of the online Transition Guide, including a list of resume dos and don'ts.

In making the transition to the civilian workplace, you need to communicate your experience, work history, and education into terms a civilian employer will understand.

Visit www.onetonline.org/crosswalk to help you translate your military experience into civilian skills.

You can download the sample resumes found in Step 6 of the online Transition Guide to help you construct your resume. There are also sample job search letters to help you with the written communication that should accompany your resume.

7. CONDUCT COMPANY RESEARCH

Research companies you are interested in working for, and investigate alternative jobs, organizations, individuals, and communities you want to target in your search. Identify specific organizations that you are interested in learning more about. Compare and evaluate the different companies by compiling information on their goals, structures, functions, problems and projected future opportunities and development.

Use social media to conduct much of your research, as described in this book. There are also many websites that are excellent online databases and tools for company research, such GlassDoor, Hoovers, CEO Express, and Manta.

The best information will come directly from people working in your targeted organizations. Use your social media channels and veteran search websites to identify them. Your most productive research activity will be communicating with them via phone, email, social media, and in person. Make a list of your networking contacts and keep track of actions taken and next steps for following-up.

8. INTERVIEW LIKE A PRO

If you want a job interview, you first need to initiate informational interviews with people in your network, such as friends, relatives, acquaintances, referrals, and new contacts. The best way to get a job is to ask for job information, advice, and referrals.

Initiate contact with a prospective employer by sending an approach letter or email and following it up with a phone call. Do not include your resume at this time – you are requesting an interview for information and advice, not asking for a job.

Hopefully your job search efforts will result in several job interviews appropriate to your objective and background. While the job interview is the most important job search activity, it is also the most stressful. Proper preparation will help reduce the stress level and make a difference in the outcome of the interview.

Your preparation should include developing a clear, concise, and well thought out answer to some of the most common interview questions, which you'll find on the online Transition Guide.

After the interview, follow-up with a thank you letter or email expressing your gratitude for the opportunity to interview. Restate your conversation or anything you wish to further clarify. Maintain a record of each interview. Include notes about the company and the interviewer. Follow-up later with a phone call.

9. NEGOTIATE YOUR BEST SALARY

The government sets military salary based on rank and years of service. In the private sector you must be prepared to negotiate your compensation based on your projected value to the employer. Salary is seldom predetermined, and many employers have some flexibility in negotiation.

Transitioning service members often undervalue themselves in the civilian work world because they tend to equate salary with base pay. If you've received base housing or a housing allowance, you know this benefit can be considerable. Use the Military Compensation Calculator at militarypay.defense.gov/Calculators/RMC-Calculator to determine your equivalent civilian compensation.

Based on your research and networking activities you should know the approximate salary range for the position you are seeking. You can also use websites such as Salary.com and SalaryScout to obtain salary information.

The ultimate purpose of your job search activities is to demonstrate your value to employers. Aim to establish your value prior to talking about a salary figure. Usually employers will talk about salary during the employment interview. If at all possible, keep the salary question until the end, as you should not attempt to translate your value into dollar figures until you have had a chance to convince the employer of your worth. When the salary question arises and it is the appropriate time to be discussed, your first step should be to clearly summarize the job responsibilities/duties as you understand them.

If you decide to negotiate an offer, you should establish common ground by placing your salary range into the employer's range. Emphasize your value, state why you believe you are worth what you want, and back it up with examples, statistics, and comparisons. Learn about salaries for your occupation, establish your value, discover what the employer is willing to pay, and negotiate in a professional manner.

Details about the Nine-Step Transition Process, exercises, and resources can be found at the Transition Guide on Corporate Gray Online:

www.CorporateGray.com

For more job search tips and transition advice, also visit the Corporate Gray Blog: **blog.corporategray.com**

Corporate Gray offers 3 great ways to get a job!

1. CORPORATE GRAY JOB FAIRS

Meet virtually or face-to-face with representatives from dozens of military-friendly companies at Corporate Gray's Virtual and In-person Job Fairs for the Military Community. In person events are held in the Washington, DC Metro and Virginia Beach areas. Visit www. CorporateGray.com/jobfairs for more information about upcoming events.

2. CORPORATE GRAY ONLINE

Post your resume and search online for jobs of interest among thousands posted by military-friendly companies. Apply directly to those whose openings appear to be a good fit with your skills, interests, and abilities.

Get transition and job search advice from the Transition Guide, Blog and Newsletter links on the website.

www.CorporateGray.com

3. THE MILITARY-TO-CIVILIAN TRANSITION GUIDE

Copies of *The Military-to-Civilian Transition Guide* are available at military transition assistance offices throughout DC, Maryland, Virginia, and other locations. Check with your local transition office to obtain a copy.

The military-friendly employers that advertise in the transition guide have immediate job opportunities suitable for transitioning military, and they would welcome your application and resume.

About the Author

Karin Lockhart-Durkee is the Director of Social Media at Corporate Gray, a company that connects employers with military veterans nationwide. She is also an admin and IT consultant, teacher, military spouse, mom, and community volunteer. Karin presents social media workshops to transitioning military members and spouses on installations in the Washington, DC Metro area.

CONTACT THE AUTHOR

If you have additional tips and advice for using social media in a job search that you feel should be included in this book, please share them with the author at karin@corporategray.com. The goal is to make this book as helpful as possible to transitioning service members, so constructive feedback is welcome.